FORENSICS

Please visit our web site at: **www.garethstevens.com**
For a free color catalog describing Gareth Stevens Publishing's list of high-quality books and multimedia programs, call 1-800-542-2595 (USA) or 1-800-387-3178 (Canada). Gareth Stevens Publishing's fax: (414) 332-3567.

Library of Congress Cataloging-in-Publication Data

Clues, the forensics files.
  Forensics.
    p. cm. — (Discovery Channel school science. Universes large and small)
    Summary: Examines some of the techniques forensic scientists use to gather evidence used in trials.
    ISBN 0-8368-3369-4 (lib. bdg.)
    1. Medical jurisprudence—Juvenile literature. 2. Forensic sciences—Juvenile literature. [1. Forensic sciences.] I. Title. II. Series.
RA1063.C585   2003
614—dc21   2003042493

This edition first published in 2004 by
Gareth Stevens Publishing
A World Almanac Education Group Company
330 West Olive Street, Suite 100
Milwaukee, WI 53212 USA

Writers: Jackie Ball, Justine Ciovacco, Maxine Dormer, Kathleen Feeley, Uechi Ng, Monique Peterson, Darcy Sharon, Tanya Stone, Denise Vega

Editor: Justine Ciovacco

Photographs: Cover, fingerprint, PhotoDisc, magnifying glass, TEK Image/Science Photo Library, shadow, ©Bob Krist/CORBIS; p. 5, footprint, AP/Wide World Photos, cave, Corel; p. 6, magnifying glass, PhotoDisc; p. 9, skeleton, PhotoDisc, WWII London, Discovery/National Archives; pp. 12–13, Mary Manhein working, clay reconstruction (both), Mary Manhein; p. 13, skull, PhotoDisc; p. 14, Espinoza, National Fish & Wildlife Forensics Laboratory, cougar, Corel; p. 15, nylon fiber, ©Michael Abbey/Photo Researchers, Inc.; p. 16, Carolus Linnaeus, Brown Brothers, Ltd.; pp. 16–17, blowfly larvae and maggot background, ©Jeff Lepore/Photo Researchers, Inc.; p. 17,

This U.S. edition copyright © 2004 by Gareth Stevens, Inc. First published in 2001 as *Clues: The Forensics Files* by Discovery Enterprises, LLC, Bethesda, Maryland. © 2001 by Discovery Communications, Inc.

Further resources for students and educators available at www.discoveryschool.com

Designed by Bill SMITH STUDIO
Creative Director: Ron Leighton
Designers: Sonia Gauba, Dmitri Kushnirsky, Eric Hoffsten, Jay Jaffe
Photo Editors: Sean Livingstone, Christie K. Silver
Intern: Chris Pascarella
Art Buyer: Lillie Caporlingua
Gareth Stevens Editor: Betsy Rasmussen
Gareth Stevens Art Director: Tammy Gruenewald
Technical Advisor: John P. Harrington

Printed in the United States of America

1 2 3 4 5 6 7 8 9 07 06 05 04 03

blowfly, ©J. H. Robinson/Photo Researchers, Inc.; p. 18, package, PhotoDisc; p. 19, Central Park and grass, Corel; pp. 20–21, firefighters, PhotoDisc; p. 22, microphotography, ©Fred Hossler/Visuals Unlimited, rugs, ©Rug Review; p. 23, Mitch Bouyer, courtesy of Little Bighorn Battlefield National Monument, age-advanced photos, National Center for Missing & Exploited Children; p. 24, Tollund Man, ©Silkeborg Museum, Denmark, Alexei and Anastasia Romanov, Brown Brothers, Ltd.; p. 26, Sir Alec Jeffreys, University of Leicester; pp. 26–27, DNA worker, Simon Fraser/Science Photo Library; p. 29, brushes and paint, PhotoDisc; p. 30, cats and eye, Corel.

Illustration: p. 5, boy with torch, Angus McBride.

Acknowledgments: pp. 12–13, reprinted by permission of Louisiana State University Press from THE BONE LADY: LIFE AS A FORENSIC ANTHROPOLOGIST, by Mary H. Manhein. Copyright © 1999 by Mary H. Manhein.

FORENSICS

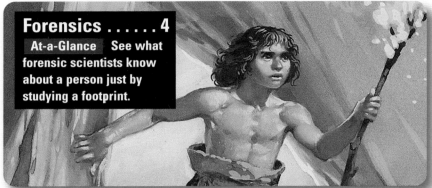

Forensics 4
At-a-Glance See what forensic scientists know about a person just by studying a footprint.

The field of forensics is large. Forensics is used to date a mummy and solve a murder. It's used to find thieves of elephant tusks and forgers of antiques. Solving almost any mysterious case relies on forensics.

Forensic scientists use scientific processes to gather evidence strong enough to be used in a court of law. Using forensic techniques—studying bones, analyzing DNA, or looking for fingerprints—law enforcement officials often discover the truth behind a jumble of information, identify victims, and catch criminals. Read on to find out how they do it in Discovery Channel's *FORENSICS*.

The mystery of Anastasia Romanov (above, right) continues. See page 25.

Final Project

Forensics

Ardeche, France, June 10, 1995

Archaeologists came across four footprints hardened in the damp clay floor of Chauvet, an ancient cave near Ardeche, France. They determined that a boy about eight years old, standing 4.5 feet (1.4 meters) tall, left the prints about twenty-five thousand years ago.

How did they know? The scientists determined the child's gender and height because they knew the footprints—8 inches (20 centimeters) long and 3.5 (9 cm) inches wide—were a typical size for an average modern-day eight-year-old boy. And the prints' indentations and skid marks told them that the boy was walking, not running.

These archaeologists determined these were the oldest human footprints in Europe by using scientific processes: observation, collecting evidence, and figuring out an answer. Forensics works the same way, with one big difference: It applies science to legal situations that often follow a crime, and sometimes it aids in historic research. But the scientific tools used in forensics are the same as those used by archaeologists.

Forensic scientists may specialize in analyzing bones, handwriting, or photographs, as well as substances such as poisons, plastics, paint, oil, or blood. But most of all, forensic scientists must be logical, careful observers of life and human behavior. And their conclusions must be scientifically accurate so that they stand up in court.

At a crime scene, the smallest detail could reveal a clue. Some of the most important forensic evidence is invisible or not obvious to the average person, such as hairs and fibers, traces of sweat or other body fluids, and fingerprints. These bits of evidence may tell a lot about a person, just as the ancient cave footprints did. But in the case of forensic science, a footprint might mean the difference between freedom and jail.

Scientists believe an eight-year-old boy left footprints at the cave's entrance.

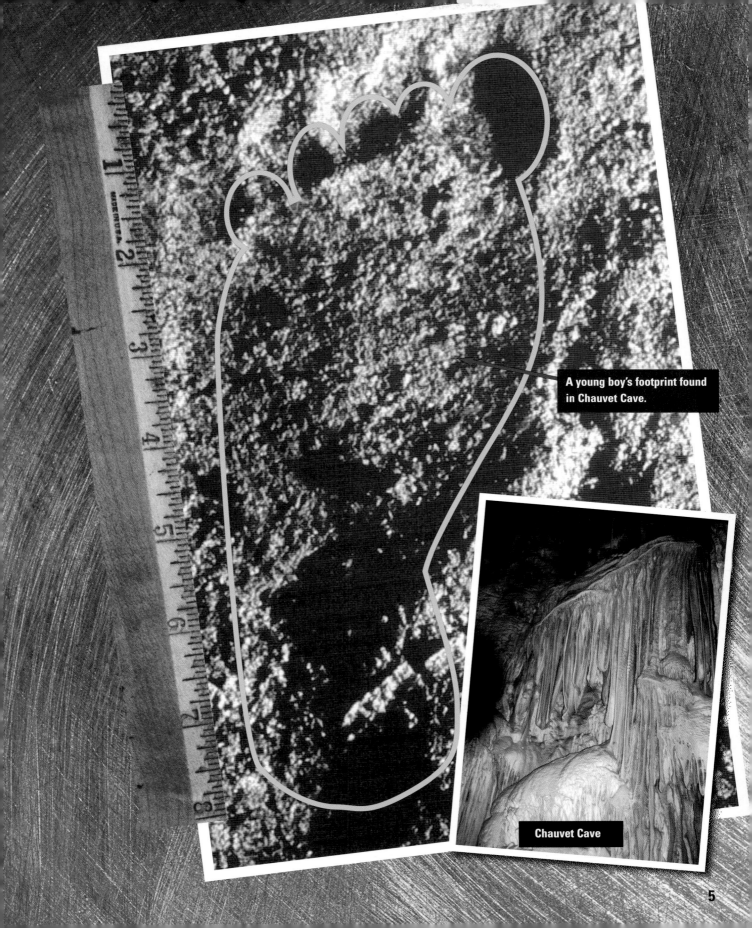

A young boy's footprint found in Chauvet Cave.

Chauvet Cave

LOOK SHARP

An interview with someone who helps you see things very clearly.

Q: You're a magnifying glass—a detective's best friend.

A: Not to mention constant companion. I really get around, going from crime scene to crime scene. Not like my cousins, the microscopes. They're stuck in the lab night and day.

Q: You must get to see a lot in your travels.

A: You bet I do. Some of it's not too pretty close-up, but it's all in a day's work. And I have to say, I do my job well in the right hands.

Q: The right hands? What do you mean?

A: I mean I'm only as good as the person who's using me. The forensic scientist, or investigator at the scene of the crime or studying evidence back at the lab, has to know what to look for. I can't do it all myself.

Q: What are some things they look for?

A: Anything and everything that could help win a case in court. Obvious things, like a drop of blood, a crack in a window, or a footprint. Not-so-obvious things, like a piece of cheese.

Q: A piece of cheese? Are we talking mice as major criminals?

A: Nope. We're talking about bite marks. Take this one crook who got so hungry burglarizing an apartment that he took a big bite out of a wedge of cheese before he ran off. Then he put it back in the fridge, leaving a perfect half circle of his choppers in the cheddar. Talk about making a first impression—ha ha!

Q: But how did his bite marks help solve the case?

A: At the lab, technicians made a wax impression from the cheese. When they had a suspect, they matched his bite to the impression. Perfect match. It stood up in court, which is the whole point of forensic science. The crook was convicted.

Q: So that's what people do in a crime lab? Impressions?

A: Among other things. In any crime lab, different experts do different things:

reconstructing crime scenes, studying human bones, examining handwriting. They can use microscopes to magnify things so they are 200,000 times bigger. It's like making a *Tyrannosaurus rex* out of an ant. The tiniest piece of evidence—even an invisible piece—can crack a case if the right tests and things are done to it.

Q: How can it be evidence if it's invisible?
A: Invisible things are only hidden to the naked eye. They can be made visible under the right circumstances. Criminals know to clean up messes they can see, but they can't clean what they can't see. And that's a lot.

Q: Why a lot?
A: The answer is contact. Every time an object or person touches another object or person, something is left behind. Sometimes you can easily see what's left, like a scratch on a car door, a fingerprint in wet paint, a piece of a note. But sometimes it's a little harder to see things like tiny hairs, fibers from clothing, flakes of dandruff or other skin, or nicks in a weapon. And sometimes you can't see it at all, like the DNA that's in every human cell.

Q: Every human cell?
A: You got it! Every single cell in a person's body contains the same DNA. So we can get DNA from skin, old toenail clippings, blood,

even sweat. And all you need is a sample not much bigger than the period at the end of this sentence.

Q: Wait a minute! Sweat is water! When the water evaporates doesn't the DNA dry up, too?
A: Correction: Most of sweat is water. But about one and a half percent is made of salts, acids, and chemicals. They stay behind, loaded with DNA. It's like finding billions of little photographs of someone, with a name attached. DNA's very convincing in court because the odds of two people having the same DNA pattern are billions to one.

Q: Wow. Anything else you want us to know? Any favorite parts of your job?
A: Let's see. I'm absolutely fabulous at analyzing handwriting, which is different for every person. I can zoom in on loops and slants and breaks in letters like nobody's business. And I'm helpful in studying blood spatter patterns.

Q: What are those?
A: Drops of blood make different shapes depending on how far they've fallen or traveled. The shapes are valuable clues to reconstructing a victim's or criminal's steps.

Q: Anything you can't do?
A: I have my limitations compared to more sophisticated magnifiers and equipment used at the lab. They can make an entire detailed history of a painting based on a tiny paint chip or flake. Or a little piece of dirt caught in a tire tread. Crime labs have huge storerooms of everyday and illegal things to compare to evidence samples: clothing materials, poisons, explosives, drugs, plastics, all kinds of things.

Q: Sounds wild. Do you ever just want to hang out at the lab and stop all this running around?
A: Nope. I like being on the road. Keeps me on my toes— and looking sharp.

Activity

WATCH THE FINE PRINT Cut out sentences from different magazines or newspapers. Tape or glue them on note cards. In these sentences, locate samples of the same word, such as "and," "the," "is," or "are." Use a magnifying glass to examine each one closely. Describe the differences you see. It is easy to find differences in handwritten documents, but today, most documents are made on computers. What differences do you think forensic scientists can find in computer-generated documents?

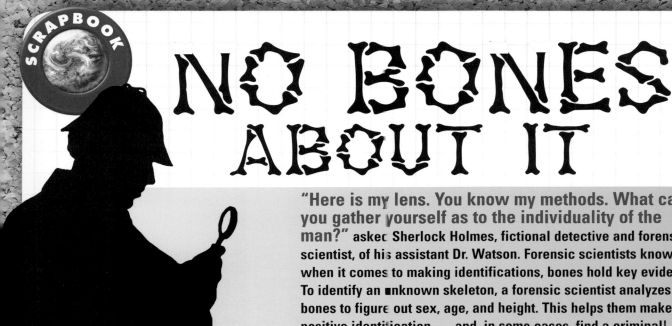

NO BONES ABOUT IT

"Here is my lens. You know my methods. What can you gather yourself as to the individuality of the man?" asked Sherlock Holmes, fictional detective and forensic scientist, of his assistant Dr. Watson. Forensic scientists know that when it comes to making identifications, bones hold key evidence. To identify an unknown skeleton, a forensic scientist analyzes the bones to figure out sex, age, and height. This helps them make a positive identification . . . and, in some cases, find a criminal!

WHERE, OH WHERE, DID MY BONES GO?

At birth, humans have 300 bones, but adults have only 206 bones. What happens to the "extra" 94 bones? We don't lose them. Bones that were once separate fuse, or join, when deposits of calcium and other minerals grow in between. Different bones fuse at different ages (see chart below). Forensic experts use this information to help determine a skeleton's age.

BONE	AGE AT FUSION
elbow	14
thigh	17
shoulder	20
clavicle, or chest	28
front of skull	40

Embú, Brazil, 1985

Dr. Josef Mengele, a high-ranking German Nazi officer, fled Germany in 1945. A forty-year-long search for Mengele (to put him on trial for war crimes) ended in a hillside cemetery in South America. Many people believed that Mengele had gone to South America and formed a new identity, but no one had proof.

In 1985 in Brazil, an international team of scientists dug up the remains of a man known as Wolfgang Gerhard, who drowned in 1979. Was Gerhard really Mengele? First the scientists established the skeleton's gender. The skull and the shape of the pelvis told them that the skeleton belonged to a male. By measuring the leg bones, they calculated that the man stood about 5 feet 8 inches (1.7 m) tall—Mengele's height. And when scientist Richard Helmer used high-tech video imaging to superimpose a photograph of Mengele onto the skull, he got a perfect match. Finally, the fate of Dr. Mengele came to light.

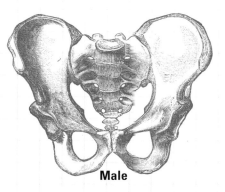

Male   **Female**

Male and female pelvises differ in shape.

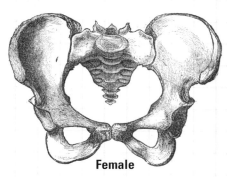

An unidentified body turned up in the remains of a church destroyed during World War II. Forensic experts examined it and discovered this victim was murdered and later placed in the rubble.

To discover the person's identity, investigators studied the bones. The size and shape of the skull led them to believe that it was a woman's. Bone fusion around the woman's skull helped establish her age between forty and fifty. But her teeth allowed them to clinch the case. Tooth enamel is the hardest substance in the human body, lasting long after all other tissues have broken down. Human teeth, like fingerprints, are unique to individuals. Investigators can make a match if dental records exist.

In this case, investigators narrowed their search to a missing woman, Rachel Dobkin. Police contacted Dobkin's dentist, Dr. Barnett Kopkin, who gave them her dental records. They matched the skeleton's teeth perfectly. Once police established Dobkin's identity, they also found enough evidence to arrest her ex-husband for her murder. This is one of the first cases in which teeth helped identify a body and convict a criminal, too.

Firefighters work in a street damaged by bombs.

WEAR AND TEAR

A bone's condition gives experts more clues to a skeleton's identity. Experts can tell if a person is left- or right-handed by examining the shoulder socket. The socket of the most used arm is usually more deeply worn, and often this arm's bones are slightly longer.

In one case, investigators were able to discover the identity of a woman who worked as a waitress because they found an odd bony ridge on a shoulder blade. The ridge was the result of carrying heavy loads—dishes and trays—overhead. Another identity question was answered when investigators found a deformity in a right knee bone, which revealed the characteristics of a man who walked with a limp after a horseback-riding accident.

9

Putting It All Together

> **I**f there are no witnesses, physical clues are all an investigator has to solve a crime. Physical evidence can surface in surprising ways.

WHO'S ON FIRST

The police or medical examiner may not be the first ones to arrive at a death scene. Insects often get there first, and their presence helps the experts determine the time of death.

A blowfly can show up as soon as ten minutes after death. It will eat and lay eggs in the bodies of large, newly dead animals. Check out the life cycle of a blowfly and think about how it can help forensic scientists measure time of death.

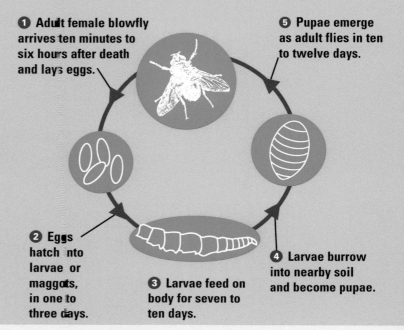

❶ Adult female blowfly arrives ten minutes to six hours after death and lays eggs.

❷ Eggs hatch into larvae or maggots, in one to three days.

❸ Larvae feed on body for seven to ten days.

❹ Larvae burrow into nearby soil and become pupae.

❺ Pupae emerge as adult flies in ten to twelve days.

TO CATCH A CRIMINAL

Sometimes criminals are caught by what they leave behind. Any piece of evidence is helpful to investigators, but the pieces don't all carry the same weight in court.

	Evidence	Accuracy	Admissible as Evidence in U.S. Court Cases
Blood	Compare proteins and other chemical compounds that vary from person to person.	Varies: One out of two people is type O. But only one in one thousand shares all nine proteins typically tested.	In all states
DNA	Compare pieces of DNA obtained from blood, saliva, or hair.	High: Except in the case of identical twins, only one in millions has the same patterns.	Varies by state
Fingerprint	Compare the pattern of ridges and whorls.	High: No two fingerprints are identical.	In all states
Hair	Compare the color, shape, and microscopic characteristics.	Poor: Can identify race but not individuals.	In all states

ANGLE OF INCIDENCE

Handwriting analysts often compare documents in a trial. A lawyer may give them two pieces of evidence—a questioned document and a known original—to look for signs that a document is a forgery, or fake. Clues include the paper's age and style, its watermarks or symbols, how hard the writer has pressed a writing instrument to paper, end strokes and letter shapes, and the original writer's common words or phrases. A handwriting analyst may use a protractor to measure the angle, or how the letters slant.

Right: Protractor evidence from two signatures; top one is false.

TEMPERATURE CHANGE

For the first few hours after death, the human body temperature drops at a rate of about 1.5 degrees every hour. This information helps medical examiners determine the time of death.

BLOOD READ

Knowing a blood type is important. If a person is unknown, blood-typing is the first step in identification. Blood-typing can also help distinguish different sources of blood. What blood type are you? Looking at the chart below, what general statement can you make about people with AB negative blood?

Blood Types of the U.S. Population

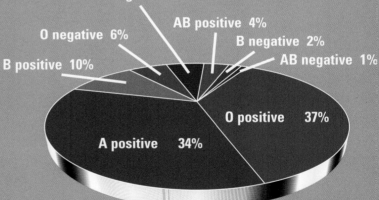

A negative 6%
AB positive 4%
O negative 6%
B negative 2%
B positive 10%
AB negative 1%
O positive 37%
A positive 34%

TIME CLUES

For the first day and a half after death, the human body undergoes rigor mortis, or the temporary stiffening of muscles due to the accumulation of waste products. Using the guidelines listed in the chart below, experts can come one step closer to pinpointing the time of death.

Rigor mortis begins at the head/neck:	1–5 hours
Rigor mortis covers entire body:	12 hours
Rigor mortis begins to disappear (body flexible, starts to decay):	36 hours
Rigor mortis cycle complete:	48 hours

Activity

MEASURING UP Mildred Trotter and G. C. Gleaser are forensic scientists who study skeletons. They have learned how to find a skeleton's height from its arm and leg bones. For an adult male of European descent, the formula is:

Length of fibula (leg bone) x 2.68 + 71.78 cm = height
Length of femur (thighbone) x 2.38 + 61.41 cm = height
Length of tibia (shinbone) x 2.52 + 78.62 cm = height

Work with a friend to measure your leg bones. Then use the formulas to determine your height. Is it close? If not, why do you think the formula did not work for your bones?

THE BONE

> I have always been drawn to puzzles. . . .
> I am fascinated with death or, more
> precisely, with the rest of the story
> that continues after death.
> —Mary H. Manhein, forensic anthropologist

You may have heard the popular saying, "Dead men tell no tales." Yet forensic anthropologist Mary H. Manhein knows that long after people can no longer speak for themselves, their bones still tell a story.

Manhein analyzes human bones to identify skeletal remains and find a cause of death. When law enforcement agencies have a mystery on their hands, and bones are all that remain to tell a story, Manhein often fills in the missing parts of the puzzle.

"Forensic anthropologists are physical anthropologists who are trained in the human skeleton," says Manhein, "and we use that training to assist law enforcement."

Mary Manhein measures a skull in her lab.

SEARCHING FOR CLUES

Bones are amazing pieces of evidence. Fortunately, calcium doesn't decay the way the rest of the body does, so bones can offer investigators plenty of information. Measuring bones can determine the age, race, weight, height, and gender of an unidentified body. Analyzing them can provide information about a person's health at the time of death.

Yet recovering bones from a site can be a tricky business, especially if they were buried years before. As Manhein says, "If you don't mind low pay, night and weekend work, treacherous recovery sites, snakes, mosquitoes,

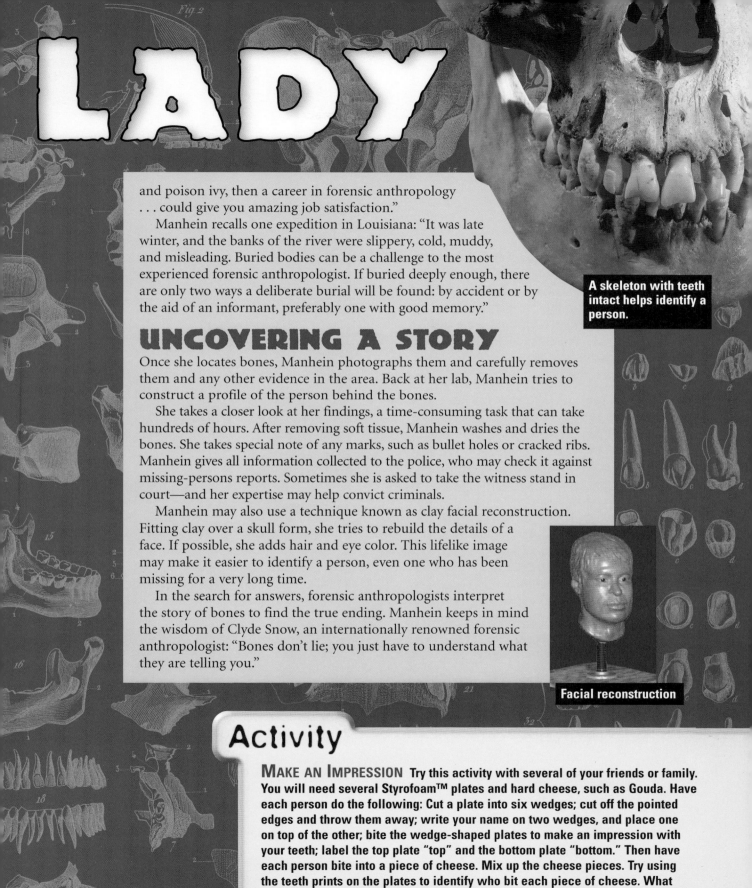

LADY

and poison ivy, then a career in forensic anthropology . . . could give you amazing job satisfaction."

Manhein recalls one expedition in Louisiana: "It was late winter, and the banks of the river were slippery, cold, muddy, and misleading. Buried bodies can be a challenge to the most experienced forensic anthropologist. If buried deeply enough, there are only two ways a deliberate burial will be found: by accident or by the aid of an informant, preferably one with good memory."

A skeleton with teeth intact helps identify a person.

UNCOVERING A STORY

Once she locates bones, Manhein photographs them and carefully removes them and any other evidence in the area. Back at her lab, Manhein tries to construct a profile of the person behind the bones.

She takes a closer look at her findings, a time-consuming task that can take hundreds of hours. After removing soft tissue, Manhein washes and dries the bones. She takes special note of any marks, such as bullet holes or cracked ribs. Manhein gives all information collected to the police, who may check it against missing-persons reports. Sometimes she is asked to take the witness stand in court—and her expertise may help convict criminals.

Manhein may also use a technique known as clay facial reconstruction. Fitting clay over a skull form, she tries to rebuild the details of a face. If possible, she adds hair and eye color. This lifelike image may make it easier to identify a person, even one who has been missing for a very long time.

In the search for answers, forensic anthropologists interpret the story of bones to find the true ending. Manhein keeps in mind the wisdom of Clyde Snow, an internationally renowned forensic anthropologist: "Bones don't lie; you just have to understand what they are telling you."

Facial reconstruction

Activity

MAKE AN IMPRESSION Try this activity with several of your friends or family. You will need several Styrofoam™ plates and hard cheese, such as Gouda. Have each person do the following: Cut a plate into six wedges; cut off the pointed edges and throw them away; write your name on two wedges, and place one on top of the other; bite the wedge-shaped plates to make an impression with your teeth; label the top plate "top" and the bottom plate "bottom." Then have each person bite into a piece of cheese. Mix up the cheese pieces. Try using the teeth prints on the plates to identify who bit each piece of cheese. What are you looking for when comparing teeth prints?

HUNTING THE HUNTERS

People aren't the only ones to benefit from forensic investigations. Animals are protected under U.S. laws, too. Poachers hunt animals for their valuable parts—an alligator's skin, an elephant's ivory tusk, or a bear's paw. Poaching is illegal because it involves hunting protected or endangered animals for profit.

So who catches poachers? It takes a team of wildlife detectives like those at the National Fish and Wildlife Forensics Laboratory in Ashland, Oregon. There, investigators have developed techniques to unravel wildlife mysteries. They also provide expert court testimony to help prevent serious violations of wildlife laws.

As soon as an animal has been killed illegally, the wildlife detectives set out to find out who did it and why. Cases where poachers kill the animal for its skin, fur, or tusks usually begin with the discovery of a dead animal or a report that someone has tried to sell an illegal item, such as black rhino horns, which can cost a buyer as much as $10,000. Even when poachers take an animal, leaving no body to be

Dr. Edgar Espinoza analyzes a skin sample.

found, investigators may hear of the case through witnesses to the crime or people to whom the poachers tried to sell goods.

However the case starts, it generally flows the same way. A check of the crime scene is often followed by calls to taxidermists—people who preserve the skins of dead animals for exhibition— or local buyers who may have seen the goods. Notices are also posted in the area to attract witnesses. Then it's off to the lab to put all of the evidence together and find answers.

Dr. Edgar Espinoza, a chemist and deputy director of the Oregon lab, explains the details from a recent case.

A cougar

A police officer brought a dead cougar to the veterinarian pathologist at the laboratory. The pathologist's job is to determine how an animal died. Depending upon what he finds, he knows which specialist at the lab to go to next for . . . expertise.

In this case, the pathologist found that the animal had died from a bullet wound to its head. He also discovered black fibers in the cougar's stomach and blue fibers in its teeth. He took the fibers to Espinoza for identification. The police officer believed the cougar was the victim of an illegal hunt, in which a customer pays to shoot a trapped animal that has been set loose just for the hunt.

Back at the crime scene, the officer also found evidence that the cougar had clawed in the snow. In two locations, he found black and blue fibers, which he sent to Espinoza. After looking for evidence in a suspect's truck, the officer found similar fibers. Espinoza believes they were probably from ropes used to tie up the cougar.

I mainly used two instruments to test the fibers. The first machine filters light and allows me to match up the exact patterns of a fiber. And both instruments allow me to analyze the chemical composition and the patterns of the materials. With these tests, I was able to make an identification of the fibers and determine that all of the fibers matched up. By having samples to test from the truck, both locations, and the cat itself, I knew that the suspect was present at both locations.

Espinoza's conclusion was correct. The evidence showed that the suspect had trapped and tied up the cougar. The cougar chewed through the ropes and managed to break free, but the suspect caught it, drove it to another location, and tied it up a second time. After being set free, the cougar was killed by a paying hunter.

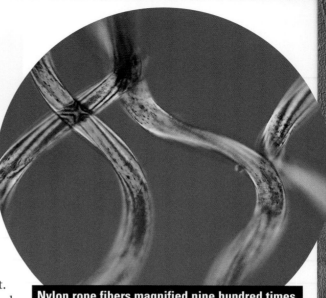

Nylon rope fibers magnified nine hundred times.

In this case, I was able to link the fibers that were tied to the crime scenes to the fibers found in the body of the cougar to the fibers found in the back of the suspect's pickup truck.

With Espinoza's fiber analysis, the suspect was arrested. Case closed.

Every case is like a triangle. One side of the triangle is the crime scene, another the victim, and the third side is the suspect. If you match up the three sides of the triangle, the case can be solved.

Activity

FIBER OPTICS Even without sophisticated labs and equipment, you can observe differences in fibers and hairs. Collect five or six samples from your home, possibly including fibers from two different rugs, loose pet hair, samples from clothing, a strand of your own hair, and fiber from a pillow. Lay the samples on a white surface and study them under a magnifying glass. Create an evidence log, and list all the characteristics you see: color, thickness, shape, texture, and other observations. Would you be able to tell the fibers apart if you didn't know their source?

BUGS IN THE

Bugs do things that may surprise you. Forensic entomology (en toe MOL o gee) is the study of insects in order to solve mysteries. Bugs—especially flies—are a welcome addition to the forensic scientist at any crime scene.

1200s

Chinese "death investigator" Sung Tz'u uses his knowledge of fly behavior to solve a murder. Tz'u has everyone in the small village show their sickles (below), or long, curved knives used for cutting long grass. None of the villagers' sickles shows any obvious signs of blood. But when Tz'u releases flies, they buzz around one sickle, picking up the scent of blood. Faced with this evidence, the guilty person confesses and is recorded in the first documented forensic entomology case.

1668

Scientist Francesco Redi disproves the notion that maggots (below) automatically appear when red meat rots. Redi places meat in jars; he covers some completely, some with wire mesh, and some he leaves open. He finds that uncovered meat attracts flies, which then lay their eggs. The eggs produce maggots after one to three days. Redi's experiment has an unexpected result: Flies can be helpful in determining a time of death. Because their life cycles are associated with the rate of decay, researchers can check bodies for the presence of maggots.

1750s

Between the 1750s and the 1780s, Carolus Linnaeus (below) publishes a classification system using standardized names for plants and animals, including different types of flies. Crime researchers can use this system to decide on the location of a murder because each fly species lives in a specific habitat.

1855

Workers fixing a house in Paris, France, find a body in a wall. The prime suspects are the current residents, but they insist they are innocent. To find out when the body was placed there, France's finest coroner, Dr. Bergeret d'Arbois, studies the body. He finds fly larvae of flesh flies and mites that would have been laid more than a year earlier. D'Arbois agrees that the residents are innocent: The body was sealed inside the wall before they moved into the house.

SYSTEM

Greenbottle blowfly

1894

Dr. Jean-Pierre Megnin publishes his book *The Fauna of Corpses*. He presents eight stages of decomposition for a body, as well as the kinds of bugs each stage attracts. For example, blowflies are the first bugs on the scene, and beetles come next because they feed on blowfly larvae. Megnin's research helps scientists determine times of death. It also helps them learn if a body has been moved or buried days after death. Megnin claims that an exposed body will attract blowflies, but a buried body attracts only flesh flies.

1935

Two bodies are found near Edinburgh, Scotland. Dr. Alexander Mearns of Glasgow University identifies the species of maggot found near the bodies, noting that they are in the third larval stage. He records how long it takes the maggots to become flies. With this information, he determines that the victims died two weeks earlier. This matches witness statements and supports other evidence, and a suspect is convicted in court.

1986

Forensic entomologist Kenneth Smith writes *A Manual of Forensic Entomology*, the first textbook devoted to this science. For the first time, information on the use of insects in forensics is made widely available, helping train people entering the field. Although the use of forensic entomology dates back many centuries, in the past, people could learn about it only through specialized journals and magazine articles.

THE FAUNA OF CORPSES

Activity

MAKING PROGRESS Research the history of developments in one of these fields: fingerprinting, DNA analysis, ballistic forensics, forensic entomology, and wildlife forensics. Compare the date the method was first used and note how it has become more sophisticated.

REAL
Strange Cases

Some cases are solved in creative ways. Here are two true stories with surprising details.

SCRAPS OF PAPER LEAD INVESTIGATORS TO BOMBER

Clementine Chapman made the mistake of opening a package mailed to her husband, James, chairman of the Wood County Board of Supervisors. The package exploded, killing her and injuring her husband.

At the crime scene, investigators found scraps of paper from the parcel's wrapping. It had faint traces of the handwritten address and a postmark that showed it came from the mailbox of Thoral Moen, whom police questioned. Moen denied sending the package; he said that anyone could have placed the box in his mailbox. Moen was cleared as a suspect.

John Tyrell, an examiner of questioned documents, put the paper fragments together. The address read. "J. A. Chapman, R.1., Marsfilld, Wis." The handwriting was so odd-looking that at first Tyrell thought it was purposely disguised. Misspelling the town's name suggested that the writer sounded out the word. But the experienced investigator decided that the writer was foreign—probably Swedish.

Only one Swede, John Magnuson, lived in the area—less than 2 miles (3 km) from Moen's mailbox. Neighbors said they saw Magnuson argue with Chapman often about running a drainage ditch through Magnuson's land.

The Burden of Proof

Examining the paper scraps, Tyrell saw that the bomber had used a medium smooth-pointed fountain pen with a unique ink mixture of black and blue-black. Investigators later found a pen with those details on Magnuson's farm.

Then on December 30, officers visiting Magnuson's farm found particles of white elm wood similar to those in the bomb particles. They arrested Magnuson and gave his handwriting samples to Tyrell.

Two other handwriting experts analyzed the writing. They agreed with Tyrell that it was Magnuson's. To further prove Magnuson's guilt, J. H. Stromberg, professor of Swedish at the University of Minnesota, testified in court that the *sh* sound does not occur in Swedish. So the word "Marsh" would be spelled Mars, "especially by poorly educated Swedes," he said. Combinations of the letters *ie* are also uncommon in Swedish, which explained the other address misspelling. A jury found Magnuson guilty, and he received a life sentence.

PIECES OF GRASS DESTROY A PHONY ALIBI

While walking his dog in New York's Central Park (right), Fridolph Trieman found the body of a strangled woman. She had no handbag or money, so police thought she might have been a victim of a robbery gone wrong. Still, the gold chain around her neck made them search for more clues.

Late that night, the woman was identified as Louise Almodovar, a young waitress from the Bronx, New York. Her parents had reported her missing the previous day. They said their daughter had married Anibal Almodovar five months earlier, but that she had left him recently.

When the police told Almodovar what had happened to his wife, he denied having anything to do with her death.

Evidence to the Contrary

The medical examiner found that Louise died between 9:00 and 10:00 P.M. on November 1. Dozens of witnesses could testify that Almodovar was at a dance hall at that time. But then Louise's parents gave police threatening letters Almodovar had written to their daughter. The police believed this evidence meant he was a suspect. Officers visited the dance hall, which was just a few hundred yards from the murder scene. They decided Almodovar could have slipped out of the dance hall, gone to the park where he may have arranged to meet his wife, killed her, and then returned to the dance hall unnoticed.

The chief of the Chemical and Toxicological Laboratory examined enlarged crime scene photos. He noticed that the body was lying in an unusual type of grass. An investigator had found the same type of grass seeds in Almodovar's pockets and trouser cuff, yet Almodovar told police he had not visited the park in more than two years. He suggested that any seeds in his pockets must have come from a recent visit to another park in the Bronx.

Joseph J. Copeland, professor of botany and biology at City College, later testified in court that the grass in question was extremely rare: It grew only in two spots on Long Island and three in Westchester County. However, it also grew in parts of Central Park, including the hill where Louise was found.

Almodovar panicked and told investigators he suddenly remembered walking in Central Park in September. Copeland was again questioned and his answer sent shock waves throughout the courtroom. The kind of grass in Almodovar's pockets and cuffs didn't bloom until mid-October.

Faced with the evidence and feeling trapped in his lies, Almodovar confessed that he'd killed his wife in a fit of rage. The grass seeds had sown the truth and brought his guilt to the surface.

Activity

CHEMICAL ANALYSIS Sometimes chemical studies help solve a crime. Try this kind of analysis by comparing a substance left at the "crime scene" with some known samples. Collect six different kinds of powder, such as salt, cornstarch, sugar, powdered sugar, and powered milk. Don't look while a friend selects one as the sample, and then see if you can identify it. Note the characteristics of the substance, and analyze each of the samples. What kinds of tests may help you gain more information? Which one matches the substance your friend selected? Make a table of each substance's characteristics.

FLY ON THE SMOLDERING WALL

The scene of a suspected arson is no place for a kid. You'd have to be pretty tiny—almost invisible—to go behind-the-scenes and watch all of the frantic activity and careful investigating that goes on once a fire has been contained.

POOF! You're an innocent fly, quietly nibbling on some trash outside a pizza shop in a shopping center.

BOOM! A nearby computer store's windows break open, spewing glass, black smoke, and hot, red flames into the air and onto the street. Minutes later, as the fire roars, police cars and fire trucks speed up to the scene. An officer starts snapping photos of the fire with a 35-mm camera as firefighters tend to the flames.

A CLOSER LOOK

Though it seems like an eternity, only half an hour has passed. Firefighters are leaving the computer store, which is now just a massive pile of charred, smoldering remains. It's a sad sight.

But one man on the scene looks pretty energized. Wearing a suit and long gray trench coat, he's walking briskly from officer to officer, giving orders and jotting things down in a small notebook. Besides a small tape recorder, which he talks into from time to time, he holds what appears to be a piece of ripe fruit. He keeps biting into it. A juicy fruit would really hit the spot right now. You fly toward him. You're on the case.

But so is he—only his case is more serious. This guy is the lead investigator. He's talking to a young woman, who appears to be a rookie officer. You listen as he and the rookie discuss what the first responders, the officers who arrived first on the scene, told her.

She says the first responders noted the flames' color and height. They also gave her a list of items found in and around the building and confirmed that no one was inside at the time of the fire. The rookie adds that she just finished interviewing two witnesses, who said they heard an explosion at 5 A.M.

"The damage is pretty even across the site," says the investigator. "Seems like the entire building started burning at once. Could be an indication of arson. An accidental fire usually starts in one location and builds out from there."

You fly in front of him, checking out the door, which doesn't look damaged. "No signs of forced entry," he says. "That's a clue to arson."

"I smell gasoline," says the rookie, writing her observation in her notes.

INSIDE INFORMATION

The investigator pulls on his gloves and slides a mask over his mouth and nose. "Let's go in," he says.

FLASH! FLASH! FLASH! A camera goes off numerous times when you fly inside. But no one's interested in getting your picture. The officer with the camera is snapping photos. He's taking close-up pictures of the ash on the counters and floor as well as the most badly burned objects.

The investigator surveys the scene. He digs into the ashes with a shovel, placing ash and burnt items in containers.

"What are those stains?" the rookie asks, pointing to a small maze of trails crisscrossing the floor.

"Fire trailers," says the investigator. "That's where an accelerant—some kind of fuel—spilled. We need to trace these paths and examine the patterns."

The investigator pulls out a device that looks like a flashlight with a wand attached to it. "Hydrocarbon detector," the investigator explains. "This will identify gasoline components, but it can't tell us whether an accelerant was there before the fire."

"Can anything do that?"

WOOF! WOOF! A large Labrador retriever on a leash and an officer enter the building.

"An arson dog can come close," says the investigator. "It'll sniff every inch of this place to find out where the gasoline odor is strongest. We'll get our best samples that way. Arson canines are trained to alert their handler when they smell certain smells—in the case of an arson, it's accelerant."

You follow the investigator and rookie into the next room. The investigator takes a notebook out of his pocket and sketches the layout of the room, indicating the location of objects and burned areas. He also makes notes about where the fire did the most damage and the location and smell of the smoke.

"The windows were blasted out," says the investigator. "The intensity of fast-moving fires can do this. A slower, smoldering fire would crack the windows in a spider-web pattern."

The investigator picks up a piece of glass. "Notice there isn't any glazing from smoke? That's because the fire hit too fast."

"Ah, and fires started with an accelerant are fast-burning," she says.

The investigator bends down and feels the ashes, noting their color and density. You fly over the site, marveling at all the glass tubes and plastic bags containing evidence, and realize that the investigation isn't over.

Now the investigator with the fruit and another detective are huddled in a corner, discussing who will follow up with the owners of the store, witnesses, and insurance agents.

Suddenly, the investigator announces he's going back to the office. Hmm. Sounds interesting. You fly out the door with him, hoping for a nibble of fruit or more information about the investigation.

Activity

HAZARD A GUESS Arson investigators must determine if a fire was purposely set or if it happened by accident. Look around your home or classroom. Are there any fire hazards? If an electrical fire occurred, what evidence would it leave behind? If the fire began on the kitchen stove and spread from there, what evidence would be left behind? Think of two other fire-starting scenarios and the evidence they would leave behind. Display all your results in a two-column chart.

Flash 'n' Show

Photographs may bring out clues that investigators couldn't uncover on their own. From documenting a car accident to recording the details of a bite mark, forensic photography goes beyond written reports to bring investigators hard evidence.

As one of the first investigators at a crime scene, a forensic photographer provides a permanent visual record of the scene. But forensic photography is not used just at crime scenes. Lab technicians also take photos to analyze evidence.

Ready for a Close-Up

Lab investigators look for clues in the tiniest details. They may use a lens or a microscope to produce enlarged pictures that show details that are otherwise invisible. The photos can capture an object's serial number, compare pieces of broken evidence, or reveal forged writing. This technique can also help investigators examine other kinds of evidence—strands of hair, fiber samples, dust, blood, and pieces of glass.

Magnified ninety-two times, a human hair may provide clues to a person's health.

Light Brights

Some clues are beyond the range of what the human eye can see. Ultraviolet, or UV, photography helps researchers see "hidden" changes: stains and chemicals on fabrics, fingerprints on multicolored surfaces, ink in documents. It also shows bite marks, cuts, scratches, and scars. UV photography creates a high-resolution picture of skin showing things not visible to the naked eye.

In the photographs at right, repairs made to a valuable antique rug show up as lighter patches because they have absorbed ultraviolet light. This may indicate a forger's attempt to blend newer synthetic yarns in with the antique natural dyes.

Original

UV photograph

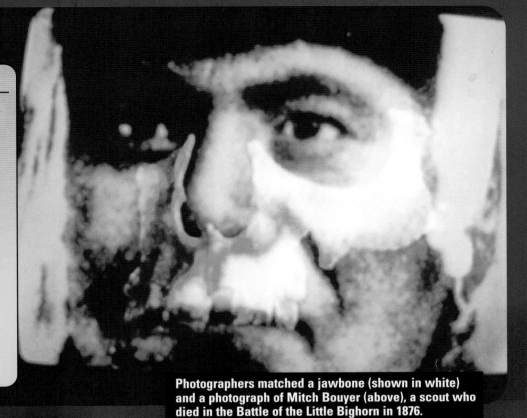

Super Sizing

It may look spooky, but superimposed photography is a huge help in identifying a missing person. It allows investigators to compare a person in a photograph to a skull or skull fragments. Using video cameras and a monitor, a technician lays an image of one object on top of another to see if the photograph and the skull match up. Unless it's a perfect match, investigators keep searching.

Photographers matched a jawbone (shown in white) and a photograph of Mitch Bouyer (above), a scout who died in the Battle of the Little Bighorn in 1876.

Changing Faces

Children's bones grow dramatically in a short period of time. To help investigators find a child who has been missing for a long period of time, they may use age-progressed photos to "see" into the future. Using the most recent photo of a child and photos of older family members, computer technicians can make the child age in a photo, showing a thinner face, a larger jaw, laugh lines, or other changes in appearance.

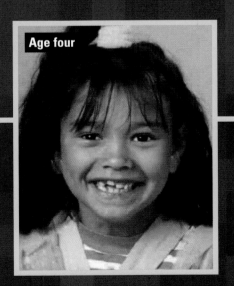

Age four

Age eighteen

An age-progressed photograph (right) shows what a four-year-old girl might look like at age eighteen.

Digging for Information

In many ways, forensics and archaeology go hand in hand.

In seeking criminals, forensic investigators use the same techniques—analyzing DNA, bones, and personal belongings—archaeologists use to learn about the past. So advancements in forensic-based investigative techniques often help archaeologists.

When scientists dig up a body, one of the most important things they need to know is how old it is. They get their answer using radiocarbon dating. Every living organism contains carbon, some of which—carbon 14—is radioactive and decreases over time. Scientists can measure how long ago an organism died by how much carbon 14 remains. The sites on this map offer cases in which researchers have used forensic techniques to uncover the mysterious identities of buried bodies.

 Jamestown, Virginia

Historians and archaeologists have been searching for evidence of England's first American colony for years. In 1994, members of the Association for the Preservation of Virginia Antiquities uncovered burnt pieces of wood dating back to sometime in the late 1500s or the early 1600s. A massive fire occurred in Jamestown in 1608, and the pieces of wood were prime evidence. Also, careful analysis of two skeletons revealed their ages, heights, races, and genders, which linked them to two settlers of the colony.

 Southwest corner of Colorado

Recent discoveries of Anasazi Indian skeletons provide significant evidence that the Anasazi may have resorted to cannibalism, eating their enemies or each other during periods of food shortages. Dated between 900 and 1000 A.D., the bones showed the same distinct knife and scrape marks found on the bones of animals the Anasazi ate. Chemical analysis of tools, pots, and human waste found near the skeletons also showed traces of human remains.

North America

South America

Anasazi cliff dwellings in Mesa Verde, Colorado.

Arica, Chile

Archaeologists found several mummies here in 1993 and identified them as the Chinchorro people, who lived nearly seven thousand years ago. Lab tests on the bones showed that the Chinchorros' diet was mainly seafood and that many of the males had unusual bony growths in their ears. From this, scientists have determined that constant exposure to cold water while fishing caused the growths.

4 Silkeborg, Denmark, and Manchester, England

Archaeologists have discovered bodies buried in bogs, or wetland areas. One such person is Tollund Man, found in Denmark in 1952. Radiocarbon dating indicated he may have been buried for two thousand years. A rope around his neck suggests that Tollund Man was hanged. Archaeologists believe that Tollund Man and dozens of other bodies nearby were victims of a mass sacrificial ritual.

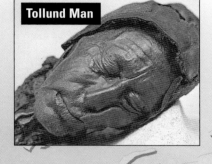

Tollund Man

Archaeologists uncovered another bog person near Manchester, England. Radiocarbon dating showed that this body was fifteen hundred years old. Unlike those found in Denmark, this person died from multiple injuries. Researchers believe he was also sacrificed in a ritual.

5 Yekaterinburg, Russia

The members of Russia's last royal family—Czar Nicolas Romanov II, his wife, and five children—were killed in 1918. Six decades later, some of their remains came to light. Scientists used forensic techniques to establish the identities of the skeletons, including superimposing photos of the family members over pictures of the skulls. The skeletons matched all of the Romanovs in age and gender except for the two youngest children, Alexei and Anastasia, whose remains have never been found.

Alexei and Anastasia Romanov

Europe

Asia

Africa

Australia

6 Tarim Basin, Central Asia

Asian folklore tells of Caucasians—tall, blue-eyed people with fair hair—traveling thousands of miles from Europe to Asia. Scholars had discarded the accounts as fantasy, but the discovery of mummies dating from 1800 B.C. in the Tarim Basin suggests otherwise. Close studies of the skull shapes, plaid clothing, and hair color, as well as DNA analysis led researchers to conclude that the mummies were indeed Europeans.

7 An Loc, Vietnam

The U.S. government received remains from a fighter jet shot down over Vietnam in 1972. An examination showed the skeleton may have been that of Lt. Michael Blassie, a soldier reported missing. But officials couldn't be sure. In 1998, Blassie's family requested the newly created DNA analysis test, which confirmed that the remains were indeed Lt. Blassie's.

Activity

CHARTING A SOURCE Archaeologists use a variety of methods to piece together the past. Each method produces different evidence. Create a chart that matches forensic techniques (e.g., DNA analysis, carbon dating, photography) with the types of information each method reveals (e.g., gender, cause of death, diet). How do these different techniques support each other? Can these techniques provide contradictory evidence?

DNA DYNAMO

The good old police car may one day carry a new high-tech item: a DNA analyzer. An officer will gather a DNA sample from inside a suspect's cheek, run it through a scanner, and in a matter of minutes have information about the suspect's unique genetic structure. Law enforcement officials around the world who receive this DNA data will be able to match it to samples of saliva or other body fluids at the scenes of unsolved crimes. This amazing technique can be traced to the work of Dr. Alec Jeffreys.

Jeffreys discovered that human genes contain a pattern of marks unique to each person, except in the case of identical twins. He developed a method, called DNA typing, to convert the marks into a readable code that can be loaded into a computer database. Investigators can check one genetic "fingerprint" against millions of others, easily linking suspects to crimes they may have committed. Because the marks are distinct from person to person, the technique has been nicknamed DNA fingerprinting.

DNA fragments are visible in ultraviolet light.

Leicester, England, 1984

To make a DNA fingerprint, Jeffreys extracts DNA from skin, blood, and even hair samples. He then breaks apart the DNA with enzymes that work like chemical scissors to cut DNA strands into pieces of different lengths.

Next, he exposes the pieces to radioactive probes that attach to specific DNA landmarks. Dark marks appear where radioactive probes attach, resulting in a pattern that looks like a fuzzy bar code.

When loaded into a computer with millions of DNA fingerprints, victims or suspects of crime scenes can help be identified. Without such technology, the probability of finding a match is one hundred million to one. (See Final Project on page 32 to learn more about the test's reliability.)

Queen Elizabeth II knighted Alec Jeffreys for developing DNA fingerprints.

JEFFREYS'S WORK IN ACTION

The murders of two women in three years frightened residents in the village of Narborough, England. The details of their deaths were strikingly similar, and police found enough evidence to arrest a suspect in 1986. Although they believed this suspect committed both crimes, they didn't have strong evidence to place him at the first murder.

The police sent blood samples from the victims, the suspect, and other DNA samples found at the crime scene to Jeffreys. His technique showed that the police were correct: Both women were victims of the same person. But the murderer's DNA fingerprint didn't match that of the suspect's. The suspect in custody was set free, the first person to be proved innocent of a crime by DNA fingerprinting.

Equipped with the real killer's DNA fingerprint, the police began the world's first DNA-based manhunt. After requesting that all local men between the ages of eighteen and thirty-five volunteer a blood sample, the police received more than five thousand samples.

Resident Colin Pitchfork had asked a friend to give blood for him. After hearing the friend mention the switch, village residents notified the police. They arrested Pitchfork and tested his blood. His DNA matched perfectly with the samples obtained from the victims. Pitchfork is now serving two life sentences in jail.

WORK CONTINUES

DNA fingerprinting was first used in the United States in 1987. Since then, more than twenty-four thousand cases have used the technique, which has cleared many suspects wrongly accused of crimes.

At the University of Leicester, Jeffreys is now working on new genetic typing techniques and exploring DNA mutations.

Activity

DNA DILEMMA Sometimes researchers have to figure out what a liquid sample is before they can test it for DNA. Try this experiment to see if you can tell a blood sample from other liquids. With an eyedropper, place a drop of red watercolor paint, a drop of ketchup, and a drop of blood from the bottom of a meat container on separate plates. (Be sure to wash your hands thoroughly with soap and water after handling raw meat.) Add a drop of water to each sample so it doesn't dry out. Next, put a Hemastix strip (available in most drugstores) in each sample. What happens to the strip? Read the directions on the strip to learn what color indicates blood. The strip, often used at crime scenes, contains chemicals that react to the chemicals found in blood.

The Case of the Dubious Dali

Scene: **Exhibit Opening, Metropolis Museum of Art**

". . . And this is a work by the surrealist painter Salvador Dali. The Metropolis Museum is thrilled to have this on loan from the Pasticcio family," announced Ms. Trixie Leed, professor of fine arts at Metropolis University and a curator at the museum.

The art students scribbled furiously in notebooks as Ms. Leed continued to discuss paintings in the "Lesser-Known Works of Great Masters" exhibit.

"Excuse me, Professor Leed," said Artie Hogarth, his nose inches away from the Dali painting.

"Please don't stand so close," said Ms. Leed. "After all, it dates back to the early 1930s."

"Well, it's just that there's some kind of hair under the layer of paint. Isn't it careless of an artist who's otherwise such a careful painter?" Artie asked suspiciously. "And there's no signature—do you think it's really a Dali?"

"Don't be ridiculous," said Ms. Leed. "The Pasticcio family has collected rare art for generations."

Head curator Madeline Fresco overheard this as she was walking past the group. "Is there a question about the authenticity of this Dali?" Artie pointed out the hairlike particle, and Ms. Fresco nodded with obvious concern. "We should inform the police."

Scene: **Forensic Lab, Metropolis Police Department, Precinct 32**

"Well, boys, what do we have?" Detective Casey Cracker asked the forensic unit.

Crime lab technician Saul Vit answered, "We used a scanning electron microscopy technique that let us break a sample of paint particles down to the micron (.00004 inch). From here we can analyze the elements in the paint pigments. Then we can easily cross-check with known manufacturers in the area and see if we get a match. One thing I can tell you for sure—the paint hasn't shown any signs of cracking or weathering. We're looking at a fairly fresh coat. The paint's chemical makeup matches paint sold around the country including at Metropolis University Art Supplies.

"Furthermore, we did a DNA analysis on that hair. The fiber is an animal hair, dated within the last few years. We are still checking to see what kind of animal."

"Any other unusual finds?"

"The original canvas was removed from the wooden frame and replaced with the forged copy. The first canvas was tacked on with nails, the second with an electric staple gun. We should be able to identify the make and model of the staple gun based on the staples and the deep impressions in the wood. We're also using iodine fuming to test for latent fingerprints on the wood. Any skin oils will absorb the iodine fumes and show up as a yellowish-brown color. I'll have results later this afternoon."

"Excellent work," praised Detective Cracker.

Scene: **Pasticcio Estate**

"Good afternoon, Detective," smiled Mrs. Pasticcio. "Please come in. I was just working in my studio."

The silver-haired octogenarian led the detective into a room filled with reproductions of original paintings. The canvas on her easel looked astonishingly like the original van Gogh mounted on the opposite wall. "It's my third attempt to master the master, so to speak," said the old lady with a giggle. "Fortunately, I get a discount on paint supplies from the university. I guess I'll always be a student, even in my old age!"

"I hate to be the bearer of bad news, but the Dali painting that you've loaned to the museum has been proven to be a forgery."

"That's impossible!" exclaimed Mrs. Pasticcio as she stroked her prize-winning Persian cat, Leo. "That painting was a gift to our family from the artist himself. How could it be a forgery?"

Detective Cracker shared the results from the forensic lab. "If you can think of anything that might lead us to the perp, here's my number." He handed Mrs. Pasticcio his card and gave Leo a rub under the chin on his way out.

"That's a beautiful cat," he said.

"Thank you," replied Mrs. Pasticcio proudly. "He's a sweetie, but no matter how often I brush him, he still sheds."

Scene: Metropolis University, Still Life Painting 101

"Sorry to interrupt, Professor Leed," Detective Cracker said, removing his hat.

"Not a problem," she said, stepping away from the fruit arrangement her students were painting. "Did you find out more about the Dali painting?"

"I did indeed," said the detective in a low voice. "We found an electric staple gun in the museum restoration department. Any chance the painting was restretched by the museum art restorers before the show?"

"Not to my knowledge,"

murmured Ms. Leed, holding a dry paintbrush up to her lips as she thought. "I supervise all the restoration at the museum and the Dali painting was already in fine condition. We kept it in storage for three months before the show. No one touched it." She removed a fiber from her lip. "Hmm, a sable bristle from my paintbrush."

"I thought most brush bristles were synthetic," said the detective.

"Yes, most inexpensive brushes are. But I use only the finest for my own work. I'm sure that's what Dali used, too."

Detective Cracker decided there was a forger and had all the facts he needed to arrest that person. What made him think there was a forgery? What evidence is important in finding the forger? Can you crack the case?

clues

Use these clues:

1. A search through the museum restoration department uncovered an electric staple gun.

2. The chemical makeup of the paint matched the paint sold at Metropolis University Art Supplies.

3. Sable bristles are not artificial.

Answer on page 32

Get a Clue!

Cats with a Cause

Scientists at the Laboratory of Genomic Diversity in Frederick, Maryland, are hoping the average kitty can help them solve crimes. In recent years, cat hair has helped convict many criminals. With this in mind, researchers are setting up a national genetic database so detectives can easily identify cat hairs on blood and tissue evidence at a crime scene. They are urging cat breeders to send in samples of their cats' saliva or blood. Their goal is to collect DNA samples from the world's thirty-three cat breeds (five breeds shown at right).

Canadian forensic experts first used cat hair as evidence in 1997. A single strand of hair from Douglas Beamish's cat, Snowball, helped convict him of a murder. The tiny hair was found on the lining of a leather jacket that was splattered with the victim's blood. The hair clearly placed Beamish at the scene of the crime.

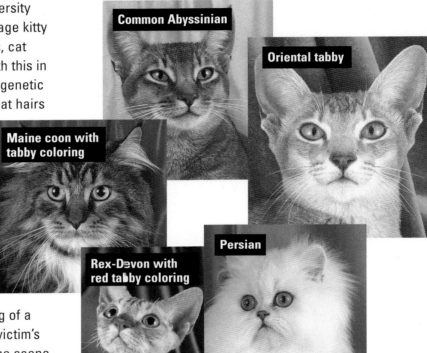

Common Abyssinian

Oriental tabby

Maine coon with tabby coloring

Rex-Devon with red tabby coloring

Persian

Eye See a Suspect

Like fingerprints, blood vessels in the retinas of your eyes have a unique pattern. Some police departments use special cameras to take photographs of the retina patterns of a suspect's eyes. These patterns are stored in a computer database so matches can be made later. This is especially helpful in catching criminals who use more than one name or who try to change their appearance.

FINGERPRINTS FOREVER

It's almost impossible to change a fingerprint. Even when you get a burn, cut, or scratch, new skin grows back with the same pattern of ridges.

Left in the Dust

The electrostatic duster is finding evidence once thought to be lost forever. A small breeze can ruin footprints left in the dust, but scientists can use the duster to replace that evidence. They place a sheet of black lifting material over the surface of a faint footprint. Then the machine pulses a high-voltage charge through the material. The electrical charge makes the material lie tightly against the surface, and the top layer of dust is transferred to the lifter. This layer offers a light copy of the foot impression.

FACT
As of 2000, there are only sixty-two forensic entomologists worldwide.

Ode to the Journey of a Fraud

In the mid-1980s, Mark Hofmann tried to sell a poem he said was written by Emily Dickinson. A master at forgery, Hofmann had done his homework. He studied the poet's handwriting and found paper stock from the poet's time period. He used a faint pencil to craft a poem about death and the meaning of life, topics common in Dickinson's work. He also signed the poem "Emily." In different handwriting, Hofmann wrote "Aunt Emily" on the back, as if a relative had scribbled her name on it. The paper bore the mark of a company that supplied paper to the poet in the early 1870s.

Hofmann found a buyer in 1985. Todd Axelrod, a rare-documents dealer in Las Vegas, Nevada, bought the work and brought it to Sotheby's, a world-famous auction house. In 1997, Daniel Lombardo, a curator at the Jones Public Library in Amherst, Massachusetts, bought the document for $24,150—money he had collected from members of the library and the Emily Dickinson International Society. When Dickinson scholars suggested the poem might be a fake, Lombardo brought it to the forensic lab of Yale University's rare book library. Their expert's handwriting analysis showed the poem was a fake.

"It's an extraordinarily good forgery," said Selby Kiffer, a senior vice president at Sotheby's. "The correct paper for the period, the correct writing instrument for the period, the literary tone was quite good—and the imitation of the writing." Sotheby's was shocked that they had helped circulate the forgery and refunded the poem's cost to the library. Hofmann has been in a Utah prison for the last decade, after being convicted in another forgery case.

DNA Decision Time

DNA fingerprinting was called "the jewel in the crown of modern forensics" by *Science* magazine. One law expert called it "a fist on the scales of justice," noting that the public seems to rely on this relatively new technique more than on any other piece of evidence. And it has enough power in some states to send a convict to the electric chair. In April 1994, Virginia became the first state to execute a murderer convicted largely by DNA evidence. Those who believe in the technique's power say that DNA fingerprinting is much more accurate than any other form of crime scene analysis of blood, skin, or hair (see chart in Almanac, page 10.)

Yet the technique is not admissible in court in all states, and it has some outspoken critics. The American Civil Liberties Union has rallied to the defense of people convicted mainly on DNA evidence. Lawyers in some cases have asked that the terms "DNA typing" or "DNA profiling" replace the commonly used term of "DNA fingerprinting" in the courtroom. They are concerned that some jurors may believe DNA evidence is as straightforward and unique as an ordinary fingerprint.

Critics argue that the genetic markers used in the technique are based on just a piece of a person's genome, which is all of their chromosomes. They correctly point out that DNA tests don't compare all of the three billion chemical units of a person's heredity. The FBI, for example, examines only thirteen of these units. Furthermore, DNA is open to contamination, so it is impossible to be sure a pure sample has been collected.

What do you think? Split your classroom into two sides—those for DNA evidence as the final word in a case and those against it. Do some research on the subject, starting with a list of cases in which DNA evidence was used. Once you gather enough evidence, have a debate. Be sure to include discussion about other evidence-gathering techniques to support your argument for or against.

ANSWER Solve-It-Yourself Mystery, pages 28–29

Detective Cracker decided there was indeed a forgery because he had evidence that a staple gun had been used on the antique painting, which originally had nails in it. He arrested the professor, Ms. Trixie Leed, for attempted forgery. The fiber underneath the paint was hair from a sable, an animal in the weasel family. Detective Cracker realized that Professor Leed always used a paintbrush with sable bristles. As a professor at M.U., Ms. Leed got all her paint from Metropolis University Art Supplies, one of the places that sold the brand of paint used by the forger. Trixie said no one touched the painting. Yet after her arrest, fingerprint comparisons confirmed that Trixie's prints matched the prints on the wooden frame, as well as on the electric staple gun in the museum's restoration department. As a fine painter herself, Trixie hoped to trick Mrs. Pasticcio by returning a fake painting in the same frame, then later selling the original for millions.

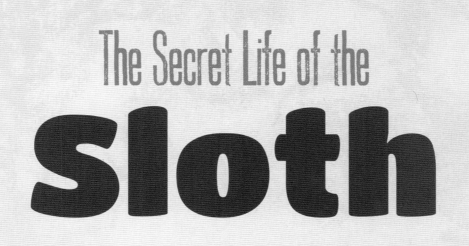

The Secret Life of the
Sloth

Laurence Pringle

Illustrated by

Kate Garchinsky

BOYDS MILLS PRESS

AN IMPRINT OF BOYDS MILLS & KANE

New York

Perezoso (Peh-reh-ZOH-soh) swims.

She swims across a narrow river to reach a place in the *rainforest* where she knows there are tree leaves she likes to eat.

She is a good swimmer, but when she reaches land, she cannot stand up and walk. Perezoso is a brown-throated three-fingered sloth, and all sloths have weak back legs. She uses her long, strong front arms to pull herself along on her belly.

Perezoso grabs a tree trunk with her long, curved front claws, then with her back claws. She climbs. She climbs up past the shrubs, vines, and short trees of the forest *understory*. She climbs higher and higher, to the top of the forest—its *canopy*. There she feels safe and at home. Sloths spend almost all of their days and nights high in trees. (This kind of life is called *arboreal*.)

Perezoso is hungry. She can't see very well so she uses her keen sense of smell to find food. She sniffs the air to find her favorite kinds of trees, with their tasty leaves, twigs, buds, and fruits. Sometimes she eats flowers.

Perezoso usually eats in the late afternoon and early evening. She chews slowly and moves slowly. She even blinks her eyes slowly! Sometimes she rests in the fork of a tree or on top of a branch. Often, as she moves, eats, or rests, she hangs upside down. She can even sleep that way, as her claws keep a tight grip on a tree limb.

Sloths are *mammals*, so Perezoso has a hairy coat. In fact, she has two—one of short hairs close to her body, and another with long, shaggy brown and gray hairs. In the rainy season, green *algae* grows on Perezoso's hair. Moths, beetles, mites, and other small creatures hide in her hair. Some of them feed on the green algae.

The algae makes her look like a green bump on a tree branch. She has almost-perfect *camouflage*. By being well hidden and moving very little, Perezoso has a secret life in the rainforest.

One day Perezoso's camouflage saves her life. A harpy eagle flies through the forest. It zooms between the understory and the canopy. With its sharp vision, it looks above and below for *prey*, hunting for monkeys and sloths. Twice the eagle swoops near Perezoso. Twice it doesn't see her.

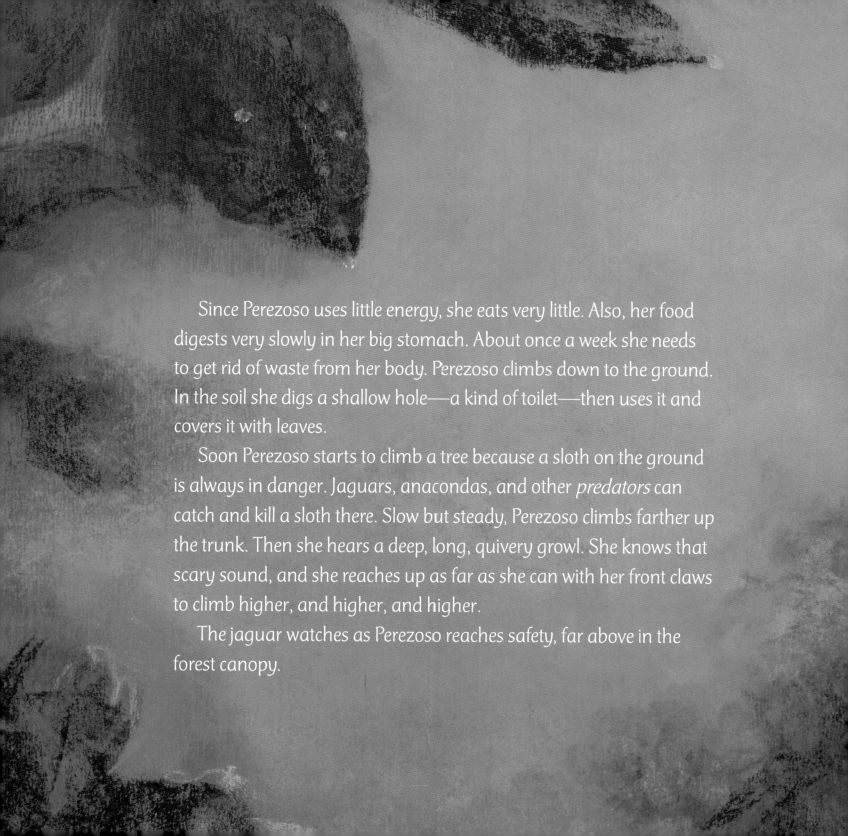

Since Perezoso uses little energy, she eats very little. Also, her food digests very slowly in her big stomach. About once a week she needs to get rid of waste from her body. Perezoso climbs down to the ground. In the soil she digs a shallow hole—a kind of toilet—then uses it and covers it with leaves.

Soon Perezoso starts to climb a tree because a sloth on the ground is always in danger. Jaguars, anacondas, and other *predators* can catch and kill a sloth there. Slow but steady, Perezoso climbs farther up the trunk. Then she hears a deep, long, quivery growl. She knows that scary sound, and she reaches up as far as she can with her front claws to climb higher, and higher, and higher.

The jaguar watches as Perezoso reaches safety, far above in the forest canopy.

For weeks now, Perezoso has had unusual feelings inside her body. Now they grow much stronger. She's had these feelings before, and she knows what to do. She climbs down to a tree branch closer to the forest floor. Beneath the branch she grips the wood with her front and back claws. And right there, hanging upside down, she gives birth to a baby sloth!

Six months earlier, Perezoso mated with a male sloth. Now she has a son, born with a full coat of hair, a full set of teeth, and strong claws. He grabs hold of his mom's shaggy hair, crawls to her chest, and begins to nurse milk.

For a few weeks the baby sloth's only food is Perezoso's milk.
He clings to her belly and chest wherever she goes.
   The baby sloth learns about his world. He listens to the sound
of raindrops on leaves, of frogs calling in the night, of howler
monkeys roaring, of scarlet macaws squawking as they fly by.
He watches and feels his mother's body as she maneuvers
among tree branches and vines. He smells a rich blend of odors
in his mother's shaggy coat and the leaves she chooses to eat.

The baby sloth and his mother cuddle close together when they sleep. After a rainy night, Perezoso moves to sunny spots where she and her baby can warm up.

He grows bigger, grows a longer hairy coat, and grows more curious about what his mother eats. He begins to take little bites of leaves and flowers.

Once the young sloth stops nursing, he reaches out to pluck
leaves to eat. By watching his mother, he learns how to smell
plants to find the best and to avoid some that are not safe to eat.

He grows stronger and bolder and sometimes moves away
from Perezoso in the canopy. But the two sloths stay near each
other. Together they clamber down a tree trunk to the forest floor
to bury their wastes or to crawl to the bottom of another tree.
Together they climb up to feed on new kinds of leaves.

One day Perezoso leads her son through the canopy to the edge of
the river. She leads him down a tree trunk and into the water—for a
kind of swimming lesson.

At first he is scared, but he watches his mother as she moves her
powerful arms and swims easily through the water. He tries. Soon he
is swimming! He discovers something wonderful: he can move three
times faster in water than he can on the ground, or up in trees.

From then on, they sometimes go for a swim, not to travel, but just for fun.

As the months pass, Perezoso does her best to give her son a good start in life. Now he is able to take care of himself. In most mammal families, this would be the time for him to leave, to look for his own home.

Three-fingered sloths are different. It is Perezoso who leaves. Her son stays where he grew up. She will live in another part of her *home range*. They touch and smell each other one last time.

In the light of a rainforest dawn, Perezoso travels
through the canopy on vines and tree branches. She
crawls out on a low branch that hangs over the river.
She lets go and splashes into the water.
Perezoso swims.

More About Sloths

In this book, the mother sloth is named Perezoso (Peh-reh-ZOH-soh) because that word is Spanish for "sloth." The actual species name of the brown-throated three-fingered sloth (sometimes called three-toed) is *Bradypus variegatus*. *Bradypus* comes from Greek and means "slow foot."

Among humans, "slothful" is a synonym for "lazy." However, sloths are not lazy. Slow, yes, but that does not make them lazy. Moving slowly and using little energy has enabled sloths to thrive in tropical forests for millions of years.

From fossil evidence, scientists know that giant sloths lived in South and North America as recently as 10,000 years ago. A South American sloth named *Megatherium* was the size of an elephant. Sloths today are much smaller. The brown-throated three-fingered sloth usually weighs no more than fourteen pounds (about the same as a big house cat or fairly small dog).

Of the six sloth species, two have been called two-toed and four kinds are called three-toed. However, all sloths have three toes on each back foot! The two-toed name was given to two species of sloths because they have two, not three, claws on their front limbs.

Some scientists who study sloths would like to correct these misleading names by focusing on the front limbs of sloths. These limbs are used like arms, not feet, with claws that are actually fingernails on finger bones. Since sloth forelimbs are armlike, with fingers, Earth's six species of sloths could be renamed to be four kinds of three-fingered sloths and two kinds of two-fingered sloths. In this book, Perezoso is called a brown-throated three-fingered sloth.

Whatever they are called, sloths are unusual mammals, with remarkable adaptations that help them live in South and Central America. Even the way their hair grows is affected by their lives of hanging upside down. Unlike the hair of other mammals, sloth hair grows from the belly toward the spine. This helps rainwater flow off their bodies easily.

Upside-down life also affects the insides of sloths. A full sloth stomach weighs a lot, and could press on lungs and make breathing difficult. This does not happen because sloth stomachs and other organs are attached to their ribs. Three-fingered sloths also have more vertebrae in their necks than most mammals. This makes their necks long and flexible. These unusual neck bones enable sloths to reach out, turn, look, sniff, or eat with their heads without moving their bodies very much.

Highly active animals that run, leap, and fly need muscles to power their actions. Sloths are Earth's slowest mammals, so they need less muscle mass. This is an advantage, because muscles add weight. Being as lightweight as possible makes it easier for sloths to lead their arboreal lives.

The leaves that a sloth eats are hard to digest. They are gradually broken down by bacteria as they move slowly through four parts of the sloth's stomach. This process can take a month—much longer than food digestion in other mammals. Also, since they don't have much energy to burn, sloths can't keep a steady body temperature as other mammals do. At night their core temperature may drop ten degrees Fahrenheit. In the morning, they solve this problem just as reptiles do: they move to a sunny place to be warmed by solar power.

The slow, secret lives of sloths are now threatened by humans. Tropical forests are cut down for timber, or burned to clear land for farms, or broken into forest fragments by the building of towns and roads. This can create a great challenge for a sloth as it moves in its home range to find food. It faces great danger when it must crawl on land, or cross a road. It may feel safer if it travels overhead on electric power lines that run along roadsides, but many sloths die by electrocution that way.

To protect sloths, people are urging electricity companies to make their power lines safer. They also place "bridges" of rope over roads so sloths do not need to crawl across. Protecting rainforests is also vital, and that includes leaving corridors of forest that sloths and other wildlife can use to travel safely from one forested area to another.

Harmless, fascinating sloths have never been more popular . . . and now they need lots of help from people.

Glossary

Algae: simple plantlike organisms that lack roots, stems, and leaves.

Arboreal: living in or among trees.

Camouflage: colors or patterns of colors that enable an animal to blend with its surroundings.

Canopy: the upper, sunlit layer of trees and vines in a rainforest, often 60 to 100 feet above the forest floor.

Home range: an area that an animal or group of animals knows well and lives in much of the time.

Mammals: warm-blooded animals with hair or fur, which give birth to live young. Female mammals can feed their young with milk from mammary glands. Sloths, cats, cows, and humans are all mammals.

Predators: animals that hunt and eat other animals.

Prey: animals that are hunted for food by predators.

Rainforest: a forest that is home to a great variety of plant and animal life, and grows in warm, tropical climates with heavy rainfall.

Understory: a place of dim light in a rainforest where shrubs and short trees grow. It lies between the forest floor and the canopy.

More Books About Sloths

Cliffe, Rebecca. *Sloths: Life in the Slow Lane*. Preston, Lancashire, UK: Sloth Conservation Foundation, 2017.

Murray, Julie. *Sloths*. Minneapolis, MN: ABDO Publishers, 2014.

Stewart, Melissa. *Sloths*. Minneapolis, MN: Carolrhoda Books, 2005.

For Rebecca, Dylan, Rosalie, and Aiden Kelehan, who treasure their times in Costa Rica, including their encounters with sloths.
Pura vida! —L.P.

For sweet, giggly Logan. Please watch over everyone I love.
Sloth hugs and kisses —Aunt Kate

The author and illustrator thank Dr. Rebecca Cliffe, zoologist at Swansea University in the United Kingdom, founder and director of The Sloth Conservation Foundation, and author of *Sloths: Life in the Slow Lane*, for her careful review of the text and illustrations.

A portion of the illustrator's proceeds benefit the AGCS Logan Hugh Memorial Fund, and Eluna, supporting children and families impacted by grief or addiction. ElunaNetwork.org.

For information about permission to reproduce selections from this book, please contact permissions@bmkbooks.com.

Boyds Mills Press
An imprint of Boyds Mills & Kane, a division of Astra Publishing House
boydsmillsandkane.com
Printed in China
ISBN: 978-1-63592-309-4 (hc)
ISBN: 978-1-63592-381-0 (eBook)
Library of Congress Control Number: 2020931292
First edition
10 9 8 7 6 5 4 3 2 1

The text is set in Mercurius CT.
The illustrations were created with soft pastels, aqua crayons, and home-brewed American walnut ink in sanded paper.